50 Seasonal Farmhouse Recipes

By: Kelly Johnson

Table of Contents

- Creamy Tomato Basil Soup
- Classic Butternut Squash Soup
- Herb Roasted Chicken
- Rustic Vegetable Pot Pie
- Apple Crisp with Oat Topping
- Maple Glazed Carrots
- Balsamic Roasted Brussels Sprouts
- Hearty Beef Stew
- Lemon Garlic Roasted Asparagus
- Pumpkin Spice Bread
- Garlic Mashed Potatoes
- Savory Quiche with Seasonal Veggies
- Honey Glazed Ham
- Berry Crisp with Almond Crumble
- Spinach and Feta Stuffed Peppers
- Carrot and Celery Slaw
- Grilled Vegetable Salad
- Spiced Pear Upside-Down Cake
- Wild Mushroom Risotto
- Zucchini Fritters
- Cucumber Tomato Salad
- Fresh Peach Cobbler
- Baked Sweet Potatoes with Maple Butter
- Chicken Pot Pie with Flaky Crust
- Roasted Beet Salad with Goat Cheese
- Stuffed Acorn Squash
- Blackberry Jam
- Vegetable and Quinoa Salad
- Creamy Polenta with Roasted Vegetables
- Strawberry Rhubarb Pie
- Lemon Herb Grilled Salmon
- Fresh Corn Chowder
- Stuffed Bell Peppers
- Sweet Potato and Black Bean Tacos
- Maple Pecan Granola

- Gingerbread Cookies
- Classic Meatloaf
- Vegetable Curry with Coconut Milk
- Autumn Harvest Salad
- Baked Apples with Cinnamon
- Chicken and Rice Casserole
- Broccoli Cheddar Soup
- Rustic Garlic Bread
- Roasted Root Vegetables
- Blueberry Muffins
- Creamy Spinach Artichoke Dip
- Pumpkin Pancakes
- Roasted Lemon Herb Chicken Thighs
- Seasonal Fruit Galette
- Winter Squash Risotto

Creamy Tomato Basil Soup

Ingredients:

- 2 tbsp olive oil
- 1 onion (chopped)
- 2 cloves garlic (minced)
- 1 can (28 oz) crushed tomatoes
- 2 cups vegetable broth
- 1 cup heavy cream
- 1 cup fresh basil (chopped)
- Salt and pepper to taste

Instructions:

1. Heat olive oil in a pot over medium heat. Sauté onion and garlic until softened.
2. Add crushed tomatoes and vegetable broth. Simmer for 15 minutes.
3. Stir in heavy cream and basil. Season with salt and pepper. Blend until smooth.

Classic Butternut Squash Soup

Ingredients:

- 1 butternut squash (peeled, seeded, and cubed)
- 1 onion (chopped)
- 2 cloves garlic (minced)
- 4 cups vegetable broth
- 1 tsp nutmeg
- Salt and pepper to taste
- 2 tbsp olive oil

Instructions:

1. Heat olive oil in a pot over medium heat. Sauté onion and garlic until translucent.
2. Add butternut squash and vegetable broth. Bring to a boil, then reduce heat and simmer for 20-25 minutes until squash is tender.
3. Blend until smooth. Stir in nutmeg, salt, and pepper.

Herb Roasted Chicken

Ingredients:

- 1 whole chicken (about 4 lbs)
- 2 tbsp olive oil
- 2 tbsp fresh rosemary (chopped)
- 2 tbsp fresh thyme (chopped)
- 4 cloves garlic (minced)
- Salt and pepper to taste

Instructions:

1. Preheat oven to 375°F (190°C).
2. Rub the chicken with olive oil, herbs, garlic, salt, and pepper.
3. Place in a roasting pan and roast for about 1.5 hours, or until internal temperature reaches 165°F (75°C).

Rustic Vegetable Pot Pie

Ingredients:

- 1 pie crust (store-bought or homemade)
- 2 cups mixed vegetables (carrots, peas, corn)
- 1 onion (chopped)
- 2 cloves garlic (minced)
- 2 cups vegetable broth
- 1 cup heavy cream
- 1 tsp thyme
- Salt and pepper to taste

Instructions:

1. Preheat oven to 400°F (200°C).
2. In a pan, sauté onion and garlic until soft. Add mixed vegetables, broth, cream, thyme, salt, and pepper. Cook until slightly thickened.
3. Pour filling into pie crust, cover with another crust, and cut slits for steam. Bake for 25-30 minutes.

Apple Crisp with Oat Topping

Ingredients:

- 4 cups sliced apples
- 1 cup brown sugar
- 1 cup rolled oats
- 1 cup flour
- ½ cup butter (melted)
- 1 tsp cinnamon

Instructions:

1. Preheat oven to 350°F (175°C). Place sliced apples in a baking dish.
2. In a bowl, mix brown sugar, oats, flour, melted butter, and cinnamon. Sprinkle over apples.
3. Bake for 30-35 minutes until topping is golden and apples are tender.

Maple Glazed Carrots

Ingredients:

- 1 lb baby carrots
- ¼ cup maple syrup
- 2 tbsp butter
- Salt and pepper to taste

Instructions:

1. In a pot, combine carrots, maple syrup, butter, salt, and pepper.
2. Cook over medium heat until carrots are tender and glazed, about 10-15 minutes.

Balsamic Roasted Brussels Sprouts

Ingredients:

- 1 lb Brussels sprouts (halved)
- 2 tbsp olive oil
- 2 tbsp balsamic vinegar
- Salt and pepper to taste

Instructions:

1. Preheat oven to 400°F (200°C).
2. Toss Brussels sprouts with olive oil, balsamic vinegar, salt, and pepper.
3. Spread on a baking sheet and roast for 20-25 minutes until crispy.

Hearty Beef Stew

Ingredients:

- 2 lbs beef chuck (cut into chunks)
- 4 cups beef broth
- 4 carrots (sliced)
- 4 potatoes (cubed)
- 1 onion (chopped)
- 2 cloves garlic (minced)
- 2 tbsp tomato paste
- Salt and pepper to taste

Instructions:

1. In a large pot, brown the beef over medium-high heat.
2. Add onion and garlic, sauté until soft. Stir in tomato paste.
3. Add beef broth, carrots, potatoes, salt, and pepper. Simmer for 1.5-2 hours until beef is tender.

Let me know if you need anything else!

Lemon Garlic Roasted Asparagus

Ingredients:

- 1 lb asparagus (trimmed)
- 2 tbsp olive oil
- 3 cloves garlic (minced)
- Juice of 1 lemon
- Salt and pepper to taste

Instructions:

1. Preheat oven to 400°F (200°C).
2. Toss asparagus with olive oil, garlic, lemon juice, salt, and pepper.
3. Spread on a baking sheet and roast for 12-15 minutes until tender.

Pumpkin Spice Bread

Ingredients:

- 1 ½ cups pumpkin puree
- 1 cup sugar
- ½ cup vegetable oil
- 2 eggs
- 1 ½ cups flour
- 1 tsp baking soda
- 1 tsp cinnamon
- ½ tsp nutmeg
- ½ tsp salt

Instructions:

1. Preheat oven to 350°F (175°C). Grease a loaf pan.
2. In a bowl, mix pumpkin puree, sugar, oil, and eggs.
3. In another bowl, combine flour, baking soda, cinnamon, nutmeg, and salt. Gradually add to the pumpkin mixture.
4. Pour into the prepared pan and bake for 60-65 minutes.

Garlic Mashed Potatoes

Ingredients:

- 2 lbs potatoes (peeled and cubed)
- 4 cloves garlic (minced)
- ½ cup butter
- ½ cup milk
- Salt and pepper to taste

Instructions:

1. Boil potatoes in salted water until tender. Drain.
2. In a pot, melt butter and sauté garlic until fragrant.
3. Mash potatoes with butter, garlic, milk, salt, and pepper until smooth.

Savory Quiche with Seasonal Veggies

Ingredients:

- 1 pie crust (store-bought or homemade)
- 4 eggs
- 1 cup milk
- 1 cup mixed seasonal vegetables (e.g., spinach, bell peppers, mushrooms)
- 1 cup shredded cheese (e.g., cheddar)
- Salt and pepper to taste

Instructions:

1. Preheat oven to 375°F (190°C).
2. Whisk together eggs, milk, salt, and pepper. Stir in vegetables and cheese.
3. Pour into the pie crust and bake for 35-40 minutes until set.

Honey Glazed Ham

Ingredients:

- 1 fully cooked ham (about 5 lbs)
- ½ cup honey
- ¼ cup brown sugar
- 2 tbsp Dijon mustard
- 1 tsp ground cloves

Instructions:

1. Preheat oven to 325°F (165°C).
2. Score the surface of the ham in a diamond pattern.
3. In a bowl, mix honey, brown sugar, mustard, and cloves. Brush over ham.
4. Bake for 1.5-2 hours, basting every 30 minutes.

Berry Crisp with Almond Crumble

Ingredients:

- 4 cups mixed berries (fresh or frozen)
- 1 cup oats
- ½ cup almond flour
- ½ cup brown sugar
- ½ cup butter (melted)
- 1 tsp cinnamon

Instructions:

1. Preheat oven to 350°F (175°C). In a baking dish, layer the berries.
2. In a bowl, combine oats, almond flour, brown sugar, melted butter, and cinnamon.
3. Sprinkle over berries and bake for 30-35 minutes until golden.

Spinach and Feta Stuffed Peppers

Ingredients:

- 4 bell peppers (halved and seeded)
- 2 cups cooked rice
- 1 cup fresh spinach (chopped)
- 1 cup feta cheese (crumbled)
- 1 tsp oregano
- Salt and pepper to taste

Instructions:

1. Preheat oven to 375°F (190°C). Place pepper halves in a baking dish.
2. In a bowl, mix rice, spinach, feta, oregano, salt, and pepper.
3. Stuff mixture into pepper halves and bake for 25-30 minutes.

Carrot and Celery Slaw

Ingredients:

- 2 cups shredded carrots
- 1 cup celery (thinly sliced)
- ½ cup mayonnaise
- 1 tbsp apple cider vinegar
- Salt and pepper to taste

Instructions:

1. In a bowl, combine shredded carrots and sliced celery.
2. In another bowl, mix mayonnaise, apple cider vinegar, salt, and pepper.
3. Toss dressing with the carrot and celery mixture. Chill before serving.

Let me know if you need anything else!

Grilled Vegetable Salad

Ingredients:

- 1 zucchini (sliced)
- 1 bell pepper (sliced)
- 1 red onion (sliced)
- 1 cup cherry tomatoes (halved)
- 2 tbsp olive oil
- Salt and pepper to taste
- Fresh basil (for garnish)

Instructions:

1. Preheat the grill to medium-high heat.
2. Toss the zucchini, bell pepper, red onion, and cherry tomatoes in olive oil, salt, and pepper.
3. Grill vegetables for about 5-7 minutes until tender and charred.
4. Remove from the grill, let cool slightly, and toss with fresh basil before serving.

Spiced Pear Upside-Down Cake

Ingredients:

- 4 ripe pears (peeled, cored, and sliced)
- ½ cup brown sugar
- ¼ cup butter
- 1 ½ cups flour
- 1 tsp baking powder
- 1 tsp cinnamon
- ½ tsp nutmeg
- ½ tsp salt
- ¾ cup sugar
- 2 eggs
- 1 tsp vanilla extract
- ½ cup milk

Instructions:

1. Preheat the oven to 350°F (175°C). Melt butter and brown sugar in a skillet over medium heat, add pears, and cook for 5 minutes.
2. In a bowl, mix flour, baking powder, cinnamon, nutmeg, and salt.
3. In another bowl, beat sugar and eggs until light. Add vanilla and milk, then combine with dry ingredients.
4. Pour batter over pears in skillet and bake for 30-35 minutes. Let cool before flipping.

Wild Mushroom Risotto

Ingredients:

- 1 cup Arborio rice
- 4 cups vegetable broth
- 1 cup wild mushrooms (sliced)
- 1 onion (chopped)
- 2 cloves garlic (minced)
- ½ cup white wine
- ½ cup Parmesan cheese (grated)
- 2 tbsp olive oil
- Salt and pepper to taste
- Fresh parsley (for garnish)

Instructions:

1. In a saucepan, heat vegetable broth and keep warm.
2. In a separate pot, heat olive oil, sauté onion and garlic until translucent.
3. Add mushrooms and cook until soft. Stir in Arborio rice and cook for 2 minutes.
4. Pour in white wine and cook until absorbed. Gradually add broth, one ladle at a time, stirring constantly until rice is creamy.
5. Stir in Parmesan cheese, season with salt and pepper, and garnish with parsley before serving.

Zucchini Fritters

Ingredients:

- 2 cups zucchini (grated)
- 1 egg
- ½ cup flour
- ¼ cup grated Parmesan cheese
- 2 cloves garlic (minced)
- Salt and pepper to taste
- Olive oil (for frying)

Instructions:

1. In a bowl, combine grated zucchini, egg, flour, Parmesan, garlic, salt, and pepper.
2. Heat olive oil in a skillet over medium heat.
3. Drop spoonfuls of the mixture into the skillet and flatten slightly. Cook for 3-4 minutes on each side until golden brown.
4. Drain on paper towels and serve warm.

Cucumber Tomato Salad

Ingredients:

- 2 cucumbers (diced)
- 2 cups cherry tomatoes (halved)
- ¼ red onion (thinly sliced)
- ¼ cup olive oil
- 2 tbsp red wine vinegar
- Salt and pepper to taste
- Fresh parsley (for garnish)

Instructions:

1. In a large bowl, combine cucumbers, tomatoes, and red onion.
2. In a separate bowl, whisk together olive oil, red wine vinegar, salt, and pepper.
3. Pour dressing over salad and toss to combine. Garnish with fresh parsley before serving.

Fresh Peach Cobbler

Ingredients:

- 4 cups fresh peaches (sliced)
- 1 cup sugar (divided)
- 1 tsp cinnamon
- 1 tsp vanilla extract
- 1 cup flour
- 1 ½ tsp baking powder
- ½ tsp salt
- ½ cup milk
- ½ cup butter (melted)

Instructions:

1. Preheat oven to 350°F (175°C). In a bowl, mix peaches with ½ cup sugar, cinnamon, and vanilla. Pour into a greased baking dish.
2. In another bowl, mix flour, baking powder, salt, and remaining sugar. Stir in milk and melted butter.
3. Pour batter over the peaches and bake for 30-35 minutes until golden and bubbly.

Baked Sweet Potatoes with Maple Butter

Ingredients:

- 4 sweet potatoes
- ¼ cup butter (softened)
- ¼ cup maple syrup
- Salt to taste

Instructions:

1. Preheat oven to 400°F (200°C). Pierce sweet potatoes with a fork and place on a baking sheet.
2. Bake for 45-60 minutes until tender.
3. In a bowl, mix softened butter and maple syrup. Serve sweet potatoes warm with maple butter and a sprinkle of salt.

Chicken Pot Pie with Flaky Crust

Ingredients:

- 2 cups cooked chicken (shredded)
- 1 cup frozen mixed vegetables
- 1 cup chicken broth
- ½ cup milk
- 1/3 cup butter
- 1/3 cup flour
- 1 tsp thyme
- Salt and pepper to taste
- 1 pie crust (store-bought or homemade)

Instructions:

1. Preheat oven to 425°F (220°C).
2. In a saucepan, melt butter, stir in flour, and cook for 1 minute. Gradually whisk in chicken broth and milk until thickened. Add chicken, vegetables, thyme, salt, and pepper.
3. Pour mixture into a pie crust and cover with another crust. Cut slits for steam. Bake for 30-35 minutes until golden brown.

Let me know if you need more recipes or any other information!

Roasted Beet Salad with Goat Cheese

Ingredients:

- 4 medium beets (roasted, peeled, and sliced)
- 4 cups mixed greens
- ½ cup goat cheese (crumbled)
- ¼ cup walnuts (toasted)
- ¼ cup balsamic vinaigrette
- Salt and pepper to taste

Instructions:

1. Preheat the oven to 400°F (200°C). Wrap beets in foil and roast for 45-60 minutes until tender. Let cool, peel, and slice.
2. In a large bowl, combine mixed greens, roasted beets, goat cheese, and walnuts.
3. Drizzle with balsamic vinaigrette, season with salt and pepper, and toss gently before serving.

Stuffed Acorn Squash

Ingredients:

- 2 acorn squashes (halved and seeded)
- 1 cup cooked quinoa
- 1 cup spinach (chopped)
- ½ cup feta cheese (crumbled)
- ½ cup walnuts (chopped)
- 2 tbsp olive oil
- Salt and pepper to taste

Instructions:

1. Preheat the oven to 375°F (190°C). Place acorn squash halves cut-side down on a baking sheet and roast for 30 minutes.
2. In a bowl, mix cooked quinoa, spinach, feta, walnuts, olive oil, salt, and pepper.
3. Remove squashes from the oven, fill with the quinoa mixture, and return to the oven for an additional 15-20 minutes until heated through.

Blackberry Jam

Ingredients:

- 4 cups blackberries (fresh or frozen)
- 2 cups sugar
- 1 tbsp lemon juice
- 1 pouch fruit pectin

Instructions:

1. In a large pot, combine blackberries, sugar, and lemon juice. Cook over medium heat until sugar dissolves.
2. Stir in fruit pectin and bring to a rolling boil. Boil for 1-2 minutes, stirring constantly.
3. Remove from heat, ladle into sterilized jars, and seal. Allow to cool before storing in the refrigerator.

Vegetable and Quinoa Salad

Ingredients:

- 1 cup cooked quinoa
- 1 cup cherry tomatoes (halved)
- 1 cucumber (diced)
- 1 bell pepper (diced)
- ¼ red onion (finely chopped)
- ¼ cup olive oil
- 2 tbsp lemon juice
- Salt and pepper to taste
- Fresh parsley (for garnish)

Instructions:

1. In a large bowl, combine cooked quinoa, cherry tomatoes, cucumber, bell pepper, and red onion.
2. In a small bowl, whisk together olive oil, lemon juice, salt, and pepper. Pour over the quinoa mixture and toss to combine.
3. Garnish with fresh parsley before serving.

Creamy Polenta with Roasted Vegetables

Ingredients:

- 1 cup polenta
- 4 cups vegetable broth
- 1 cup heavy cream
- 2 cups assorted vegetables (zucchini, bell peppers, carrots)
- 2 tbsp olive oil
- Salt and pepper to taste
- Grated Parmesan cheese (for serving)

Instructions:

1. Preheat the oven to 425°F (220°C). Toss assorted vegetables in olive oil, salt, and pepper, and roast for 20-25 minutes.
2. In a saucepan, bring vegetable broth to a boil. Slowly whisk in polenta, reduce heat, and cook for 15-20 minutes until thickened.
3. Stir in heavy cream and serve polenta topped with roasted vegetables and grated Parmesan.

Strawberry Rhubarb Pie

Ingredients:

- 2 cups strawberries (sliced)
- 2 cups rhubarb (chopped)
- 1 ¼ cups sugar (divided)
- ¼ cup cornstarch
- 1 tsp vanilla extract
- 1 pie crust (store-bought or homemade)
- 1 egg (beaten, for egg wash)

Instructions:

1. Preheat the oven to 425°F (220°C). In a bowl, combine strawberries, rhubarb, 1 cup sugar, cornstarch, and vanilla.
2. Roll out pie crust and place in a pie dish. Fill with the strawberry-rhubarb mixture and cover with another crust.
3. Cut slits for steam, brush with beaten egg, and sprinkle with remaining sugar. Bake for 45-50 minutes until crust is golden and filling is bubbling.

Lemon Herb Grilled Salmon

Ingredients:

- 4 salmon fillets
- 2 tbsp olive oil
- 2 tbsp lemon juice
- 1 tsp dried oregano
- 1 tsp garlic powder
- Salt and pepper to taste
- Lemon wedges (for serving)

Instructions:

1. Preheat the grill to medium-high heat. In a bowl, mix olive oil, lemon juice, oregano, garlic powder, salt, and pepper.
2. Brush the salmon fillets with the marinade and place on the grill.
3. Grill for about 4-5 minutes per side until cooked through. Serve with lemon wedges.

Fresh Corn Chowder

Ingredients:

- 4 cups fresh corn kernels (or frozen)
- 1 onion (chopped)
- 2 potatoes (diced)
- 4 cups vegetable broth
- 1 cup heavy cream
- 2 tbsp butter
- Salt and pepper to taste
- Fresh chives (for garnish)

Instructions:

1. In a large pot, melt butter over medium heat. Add onion and cook until translucent.
2. Add potatoes, corn, and vegetable broth. Simmer until potatoes are tender, about 15-20 minutes.
3. Stir in heavy cream, season with salt and pepper, and cook for an additional 5 minutes. Garnish with fresh chives before serving.

Let me know if you need more recipes or further assistance!

Stuffed Bell Peppers

Ingredients:

- 4 bell peppers (any color)
- 1 cup cooked rice (white or brown)
- 1 cup black beans (rinsed and drained)
- 1 cup corn (canned or frozen)
- 1 cup diced tomatoes (canned)
- 1 tsp cumin
- 1 tsp chili powder
- Salt and pepper to taste
- 1 cup shredded cheese (optional)

Instructions:

1. Preheat the oven to 375°F (190°C). Cut the tops off the bell peppers and remove the seeds.
2. In a bowl, mix cooked rice, black beans, corn, diced tomatoes, cumin, chili powder, salt, and pepper.
3. Stuff each bell pepper with the mixture and place in a baking dish. If desired, sprinkle cheese on top.
4. Cover with foil and bake for 30 minutes. Remove foil and bake for an additional 10 minutes until the peppers are tender.

Sweet Potato and Black Bean Tacos

Ingredients:

- 2 medium sweet potatoes (peeled and diced)
- 1 can black beans (rinsed and drained)
- 1 tsp cumin
- 1 tsp paprika
- Salt and pepper to taste
- Corn tortillas
- Avocado (sliced)
- Fresh cilantro (for garnish)
- Lime wedges (for serving)

Instructions:

1. Preheat the oven to 400°F (200°C). Toss sweet potatoes with cumin, paprika, salt, and pepper, and spread on a baking sheet. Roast for 20-25 minutes until tender.
2. In a small saucepan, warm black beans over low heat.
3. Assemble tacos by filling corn tortillas with roasted sweet potatoes, black beans, avocado, and garnish with cilantro and lime juice.

Maple Pecan Granola

Ingredients:

- 3 cups rolled oats
- 1 cup pecans (chopped)
- ½ cup maple syrup
- ¼ cup coconut oil (melted)
- 1 tsp vanilla extract
- 1 tsp cinnamon
- ½ tsp salt

Instructions:

1. Preheat the oven to 350°F (175°C). In a large bowl, mix oats, pecans, maple syrup, melted coconut oil, vanilla, cinnamon, and salt.
2. Spread the mixture onto a baking sheet lined with parchment paper. Bake for 25-30 minutes, stirring halfway through, until golden brown.
3. Allow to cool before storing in an airtight container.

Gingerbread Cookies

Ingredients:

- 3 cups all-purpose flour
- 1 tbsp ginger (ground)
- 1 tbsp cinnamon
- 1 tsp baking soda
- ½ tsp salt
- ¾ cup unsalted butter (softened)
- ¾ cup brown sugar
- 1 large egg
- ½ cup molasses
- Icing (for decorating)

Instructions:

1. Preheat the oven to 350°F (175°C). In a bowl, whisk together flour, ginger, cinnamon, baking soda, and salt.
2. In another bowl, cream together butter and brown sugar until smooth. Beat in egg and molasses.
3. Gradually add dry ingredients to the wet mixture. Roll dough into balls and flatten slightly on a baking sheet.
4. Bake for 8-10 minutes until set. Let cool before decorating with icing.

Classic Meatloaf

Ingredients:

- 1 lb ground beef (or turkey)
- 1 cup breadcrumbs
- 1 egg (beaten)
- 1 onion (chopped)
- 1 cup milk
- 1 tsp salt
- ½ tsp pepper
- ¼ cup ketchup (for topping)

Instructions:

1. Preheat the oven to 350°F (175°C). In a large bowl, mix ground beef, breadcrumbs, egg, onion, milk, salt, and pepper.
2. Shape the mixture into a loaf and place in a greased loaf pan. Top with ketchup.
3. Bake for 1 hour or until the internal temperature reaches 160°F (70°C). Let rest for 10 minutes before slicing.

Vegetable Curry with Coconut Milk

Ingredients:

- 1 tbsp coconut oil
- 1 onion (chopped)
- 2 garlic cloves (minced)
- 1 tbsp ginger (grated)
- 2 cups mixed vegetables (carrots, bell peppers, peas)
- 1 can coconut milk
- 2 tbsp curry powder
- Salt to taste
- Fresh cilantro (for garnish)

Instructions:

1. In a large pot, heat coconut oil over medium heat. Add onion, garlic, and ginger, and sauté until fragrant.
2. Add mixed vegetables and curry powder, cooking for another 5 minutes.
3. Pour in coconut milk, bring to a simmer, and cook for 15-20 minutes until vegetables are tender. Season with salt and garnish with cilantro.

Autumn Harvest Salad

Ingredients:

- 4 cups mixed greens
- 1 cup roasted butternut squash (diced)
- ½ cup cranberries (dried)
- ½ cup pecans (toasted)
- ¼ cup feta cheese (crumbled)
- ¼ cup balsamic vinaigrette

Instructions:

1. In a large bowl, combine mixed greens, roasted butternut squash, cranberries, pecans, and feta cheese.
2. Drizzle with balsamic vinaigrette, toss gently, and serve.

Baked Apples with Cinnamon

Ingredients:

- 4 apples (cored)
- ¼ cup brown sugar
- ½ tsp cinnamon
- ¼ cup raisins (optional)
- ¼ cup walnuts (chopped, optional)
- 1 tbsp butter

Instructions:

1. Preheat the oven to 350°F (175°C). Place cored apples in a baking dish.
2. In a bowl, mix brown sugar, cinnamon, raisins, and walnuts. Stuff the mixture into the apples.
3. Top each apple with a small piece of butter. Bake for 25-30 minutes until apples are tender.

Let me know if you need more recipes or any other assistance!

Chicken and Rice Casserole

Ingredients:

- 2 cups cooked chicken (shredded)
- 1 cup uncooked white rice
- 2 cups chicken broth
- 1 cup cream of mushroom soup
- 1 cup mixed vegetables (frozen or fresh)
- 1 onion (chopped)
- 1 tsp garlic powder
- Salt and pepper to taste
- 1 cup shredded cheese (optional)

Instructions:

1. Preheat the oven to 375°F (190°C). In a large bowl, combine shredded chicken, uncooked rice, chicken broth, cream of mushroom soup, mixed vegetables, onion, garlic powder, salt, and pepper.
2. Pour the mixture into a greased casserole dish and cover with foil.
3. Bake for 1 hour. Remove foil, sprinkle with cheese if desired, and bake for an additional 10-15 minutes until cheese is melted and bubbly.

Broccoli Cheddar Soup

Ingredients:

- 4 cups broccoli florets
- 1 onion (chopped)
- 3 cups vegetable broth
- 2 cups shredded cheddar cheese
- 1 cup milk
- 2 tbsp butter
- 2 tbsp flour
- Salt and pepper to taste

Instructions:

1. In a large pot, melt butter over medium heat. Add onion and sauté until soft.
2. Add broccoli and vegetable broth; bring to a boil. Reduce heat and simmer until broccoli is tender, about 10 minutes.
3. In a separate bowl, whisk flour and milk until smooth. Slowly add to the soup while stirring.
4. Cook until thickened, then stir in cheese until melted. Season with salt and pepper before serving.

Rustic Garlic Bread

Ingredients:

- 1 loaf of crusty bread (like ciabatta or baguette)
- ½ cup unsalted butter (softened)
- 4 cloves garlic (minced)
- 2 tbsp fresh parsley (chopped)
- Salt to taste

Instructions:

1. Preheat the oven to 375°F (190°C). In a bowl, mix softened butter, minced garlic, parsley, and salt until well combined.
2. Slice the bread in half lengthwise and spread the garlic butter mixture on both halves.
3. Place on a baking sheet and bake for 10-15 minutes until golden and crispy. Slice and serve warm.

Roasted Root Vegetables

Ingredients:

- 2 cups mixed root vegetables (carrots, parsnips, potatoes, etc.), diced
- 2 tbsp olive oil
- 1 tsp rosemary
- 1 tsp thyme
- Salt and pepper to taste

Instructions:

1. Preheat the oven to 400°F (200°C). In a bowl, toss root vegetables with olive oil, rosemary, thyme, salt, and pepper.
2. Spread the vegetables in a single layer on a baking sheet.
3. Roast for 25-30 minutes or until tender and golden, stirring halfway through.

Blueberry Muffins

Ingredients:

- 2 cups all-purpose flour
- 1 cup sugar
- ½ cup unsalted butter (melted)
- 1 cup milk
- 2 eggs
- 2 tsp baking powder
- 1 tsp vanilla extract
- 1 cup fresh or frozen blueberries

Instructions:

1. Preheat the oven to 375°F (190°C). Grease or line a muffin tin.
2. In a large bowl, combine flour, sugar, baking powder, and a pinch of salt.
3. In another bowl, whisk together melted butter, milk, eggs, and vanilla. Add to dry ingredients and stir until just combined. Gently fold in blueberries.
4. Divide the batter among the muffin cups and bake for 18-20 minutes until golden and a toothpick comes out clean.

Creamy Spinach Artichoke Dip

Ingredients:

- 1 cup frozen spinach (thawed and drained)
- 1 cup canned artichoke hearts (chopped)
- 1 cup cream cheese (softened)
- ½ cup sour cream
- ½ cup mayonnaise
- 1 cup shredded mozzarella cheese
- ½ cup grated Parmesan cheese
- 1 tsp garlic powder
- Salt and pepper to taste

Instructions:

1. Preheat the oven to 350°F (175°C). In a mixing bowl, combine spinach, artichoke hearts, cream cheese, sour cream, mayonnaise, mozzarella, Parmesan, garlic powder, salt, and pepper.
2. Spread the mixture into a baking dish and bake for 25-30 minutes until bubbly and golden on top. Serve warm with chips or bread.

Pumpkin Pancakes

Ingredients:

- 1 cup all-purpose flour
- 1 tbsp sugar
- 2 tsp baking powder
- ½ tsp baking soda
- ½ tsp cinnamon
- ¼ tsp nutmeg
- ½ tsp salt
- 1 cup pumpkin puree
- 1 cup milk
- 1 egg
- 2 tbsp melted butter

Instructions:

1. In a bowl, mix flour, sugar, baking powder, baking soda, spices, and salt.
2. In another bowl, combine pumpkin, milk, egg, and melted butter. Stir the wet ingredients into the dry ingredients until just combined.
3. Heat a skillet over medium heat and pour ¼ cup of batter for each pancake. Cook until bubbles form, then flip and cook until golden. Serve with syrup.

Roasted Lemon Herb Chicken Thighs

Ingredients:

- 4 chicken thighs (bone-in, skin-on)
- 2 lemons (zested and juiced)
- 3 tbsp olive oil
- 4 garlic cloves (minced)
- 1 tsp thyme
- 1 tsp rosemary
- Salt and pepper to taste

Instructions:

1. Preheat the oven to 425°F (220°C). In a bowl, whisk together lemon juice, zest, olive oil, garlic, thyme, rosemary, salt, and pepper.
2. Place chicken thighs in a baking dish and pour the marinade over them. Let marinate for at least 30 minutes.
3. Roast chicken in the oven for 35-40 minutes until cooked through and skin is crispy. Serve with roasted vegetables or rice.

Let me know if you need more recipes or any other assistance!

Seasonal Fruit Galette

Ingredients:

- 1 pie crust (store-bought or homemade)
- 2 cups seasonal fruit (such as apples, pears, berries, or peaches), sliced
- 1/4 cup sugar (adjust based on fruit sweetness)
- 1 tbsp cornstarch
- 1 tsp vanilla extract
- 1/2 tsp cinnamon (optional)
- 1 egg (for egg wash)
- 1 tbsp butter (for topping)

Instructions:

1. Preheat the oven to 375°F (190°C). Roll out the pie crust on a floured surface and transfer it to a baking sheet lined with parchment paper.
2. In a mixing bowl, combine the sliced fruit, sugar, cornstarch, vanilla extract, and cinnamon. Toss to coat the fruit evenly.
3. Spoon the fruit mixture onto the center of the pie crust, leaving a 2-inch border around the edges. Fold the edges of the crust over the fruit, pleating as you go.
4. Brush the crust with the beaten egg and dot the fruit with small pieces of butter.
5. Bake for 30-35 minutes until the crust is golden brown and the fruit is bubbly. Allow to cool slightly before serving.

Winter Squash Risotto

Ingredients:

- 1 cup Arborio rice
- 2 cups winter squash (such as butternut or acorn), diced
- 4 cups vegetable broth (warmed)
- 1 small onion (finely chopped)
- 2 cloves garlic (minced)
- 1/2 cup white wine (optional)
- 1/2 cup grated Parmesan cheese (or nutritional yeast for a vegan option)
- 2 tbsp olive oil
- 1 tbsp butter (optional)
- Salt and pepper to taste
- Fresh herbs (such as sage or thyme) for garnish

Instructions:

1. In a large skillet or pot, heat olive oil over medium heat. Add the onion and garlic, cooking until softened.
2. Stir in the diced winter squash and cook for about 5 minutes until it starts to soften.
3. Add the Arborio rice and stir for 1-2 minutes until the rice is well-coated and slightly translucent.
4. If using, pour in the white wine and let it simmer until mostly absorbed. Gradually add the warmed vegetable broth, one ladle at a time, stirring frequently and allowing the liquid to absorb before adding more.
5. Continue this process for about 18-20 minutes until the rice is creamy and al dente. Stir in the Parmesan cheese and butter (if using), and season with salt and pepper.
6. Serve warm, garnished with fresh herbs.

Let me know if you need more recipes or any other help!

www.ingramcontent.com/pod-product-compliance
Lightning Source LLC
LaVergne TN
LVHW081503060526
838201LV00056BA/2902